There is only one thing to fear...
To become a warrior without fear.

BLEACH 38

FEAR FOR FIGHT

STARS AND

檜佐木修兵

Shuhei Hisagi

Ikkaku Madarame

斑目一角

Izuru Kira

吉良イヅル

plot

When high school student Ichigo Kurosaki meets Soul Reaper Rukia Kuchiki his life is changed forever. Soon Ichigo is a soul-cleansing Soul Reaper too, and he finds himself having adventures, as well as problems, that he never would have imagined. Now Ichigo and his friends must stop renegade Soul Reaper Aizen and his army of Arrancars from destroying the Soul Society and wiping out KarakuraTown as well.

The battle finally begins! The Thirteen Court Guard Companies head to Karakura while Ichigo remains in Hueco Mundo to rescue Orihime. Now the replica Karakura becomes a battlefield as Aizen's minions clash with the Soul Reapers. Barragan orders his Fracciónes to destroy the four pillars holding the two Karakuras in place, and Ikkaku, Yumichika, Izuru, and Hisagi set out to stop them. But as Kira faces off against Abirama, the Fracción suddenly transforms himself into Águila!

BLEACH ALL

ポウ
Poww

アビラマ
Abirama

Findorr
フィンドール

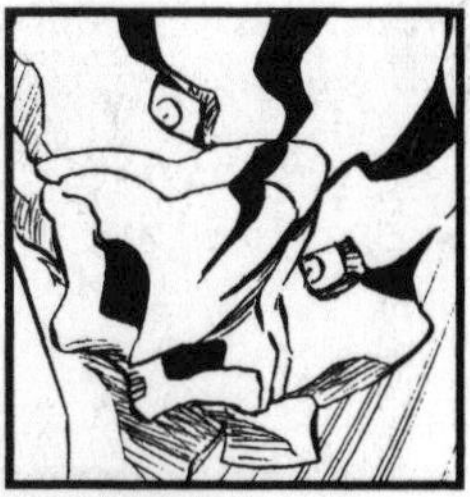

STORIES

BLEACH 38

FEAR FOR FIGHT

Contents

323. Gloomy, Ghastly, and Full of Despair	7
324. The Reaper	31
325. Fear For Fight	51
326. Knockdown Monster	71
327. Knockdown Monsters	91
328. The Knuckle Debate	111
329. RAGING RAMPAGE	135
330. CROSSING SWORDS	155
331. Don't Believe the Hide	175

DON'T BE MISLED.
THE WINGS OF ÁGUILA AREN'T NORMAL WINGS.
THEY CRUSH ANY-THING THEY TOUCH.
THEY'RE WINGS OF HEAVY STEEL!!

BLEACH
ブリーチ
323. Gloomy, Ghastly, and Full of Despair

BLEACH
ブリーチ

READ THIS WAY

SWIP
WMM
...?
ANOTHER SPELL?
HADÔ 58.
WHAP

SHWOOOO
TENRAN!!
(TORNADO)

IF THEY WERE JUST WINGS...
...COULD THEY WITH-STAND A TORNADO?
OF COURSE NOT!!

READ THIS WAY
HMPH.
YOU SNEAKY ...
RAT!!
DEVORAR PLUMA!! (DEVOURING FEATHER)
WHOOM

UGH!
THEY GO RIGHT THROUGH THE WALLS!
THERE YOU ARE!

SHAK
SHAK
TOM
WHAMWHAMWHAM

YOU LITTLE COWARD!
COME OUT AND FIGHT!
HE STILL HAS PLENTY OF FEATHERS.
THEY MUST REGENERATE INSTANTLY...
...GROWING BACK FROM THE TIPS.
THEN...
YOU'RE TRYING TO DEVISE A PLAN...
...AS YOU SCURRY AROUND.
BUT I WON'T LET YOU!

READ THIS WAY

CHAK
WHUP

HA!
NOW WHERE WILL YOU HIDE ?!

RRMMMMMMM
WHAT?!
DID THE RUBBLE CRUSH YOUR LEGS?
I CAME IN FASTER THAN I THOUGHT!
THANKS.
I NEEDED TO CLOSE THE DISTANCE BETWEEN US.
I HAD TO GET YOU TO ATTACK ME AT CLOSE RANGE.
MY BLADE...
...WORKS BEST UP CLOSE AND PERSONAL.
I DON'T UNDERSTAND!
WHAT DO YOU INTEND TO CUT WITH THAT SILLY THING?!

WHAT...
...THE...
... DEVIL ?!
KRK KRK
KRK KRK
KRAK

WOOOOO
KABOOM
UGH ...
BLAST.
MY WINGS...
IT DOUBLES THE WEIGHT OF ANYTHING IT CUTS.
IF I CUT TWICE, THE WEIGHT DOUBLES AGAIN.
I CUT IT THREE TIMES, IT DOUBLES AGAIN.
TMP

THAT'S THE POWER OF...
...MY ZANPAKU-TÔ, WABISUKE.
WHEN I STRUCK YOU...
...I CUT MOST OF YOUR FEATHERS FOUR TIMES.
YOUR WINGS ARE AS HEAVY AS LEAD NOW...
...MUCH TOO HEAVY TO FLY WITH.
YOU DIRTY SNEAK...
IS THAT HOW A WARRIOR FIGHTS?!
DIRTY?

READ THIS WAY

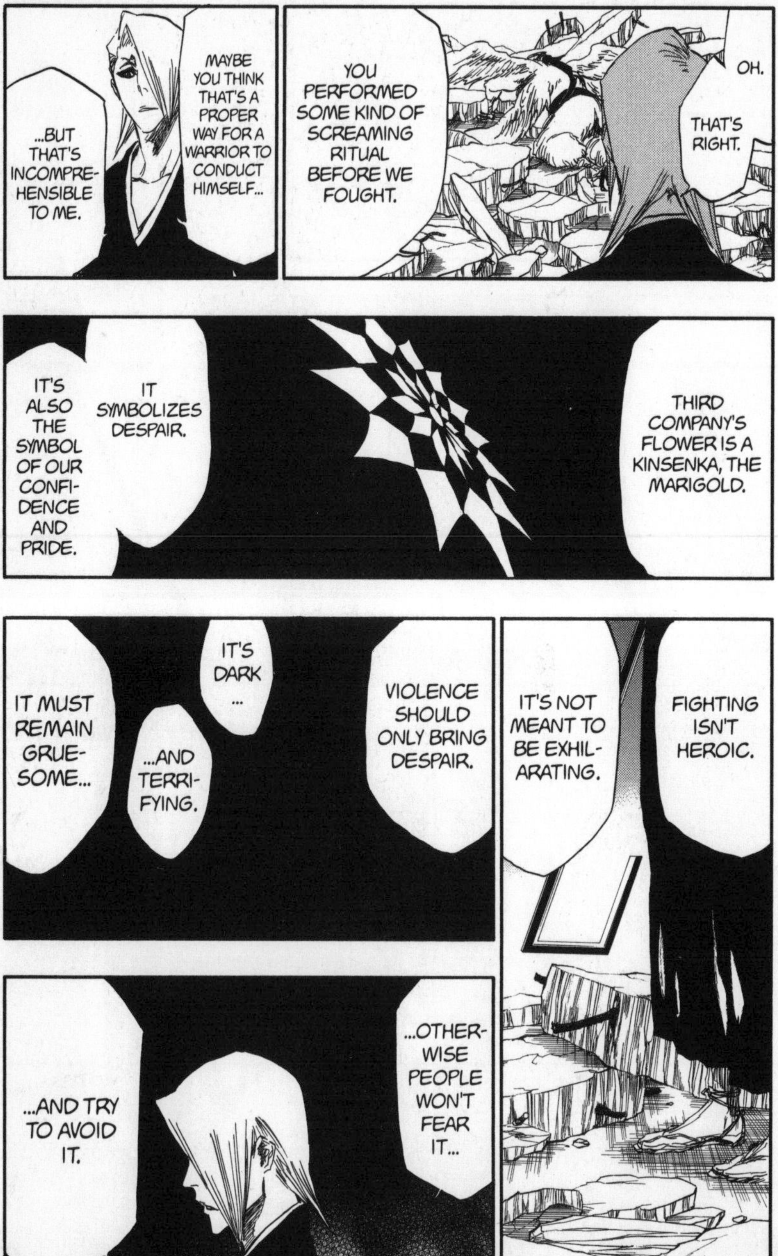

TO MY MIND, WABISUKE ...
...OF ALL THE ZANPAKU-TÔ...
...BEST EXEMPLIFIES THIRD COMPANY'S PHILOSOPHY.
IT INCREASES THE WEIGHT OF WHATEVER IT CUTS.
THOSE WHO ARE CUT BY IT ARE FORCED TO CRAWL, UNABLE TO BEAR THEIR OWN WEIGHT.
AND THEY ALWAYS ...
...BOW THEIR HEADS...
...AS IF ASKING FOR FORGIVE-NESS.
THAT'S WHY IT'S CALLED ...
...WABISUKE.
(APOLOGY)
YOU ASKED WHAT I INTENDED TO CUT...
...WITH THIS SILLY-LOOKING BLADE.

CHAK
A WAR-RIOR ...
...SHOULD NEVER BEG FOR HIS LIFE.
W—
WAIT!
SHAK

324. The Reaper

...THAT YOU'LL NEVER FORGIVE ME.
KLIK

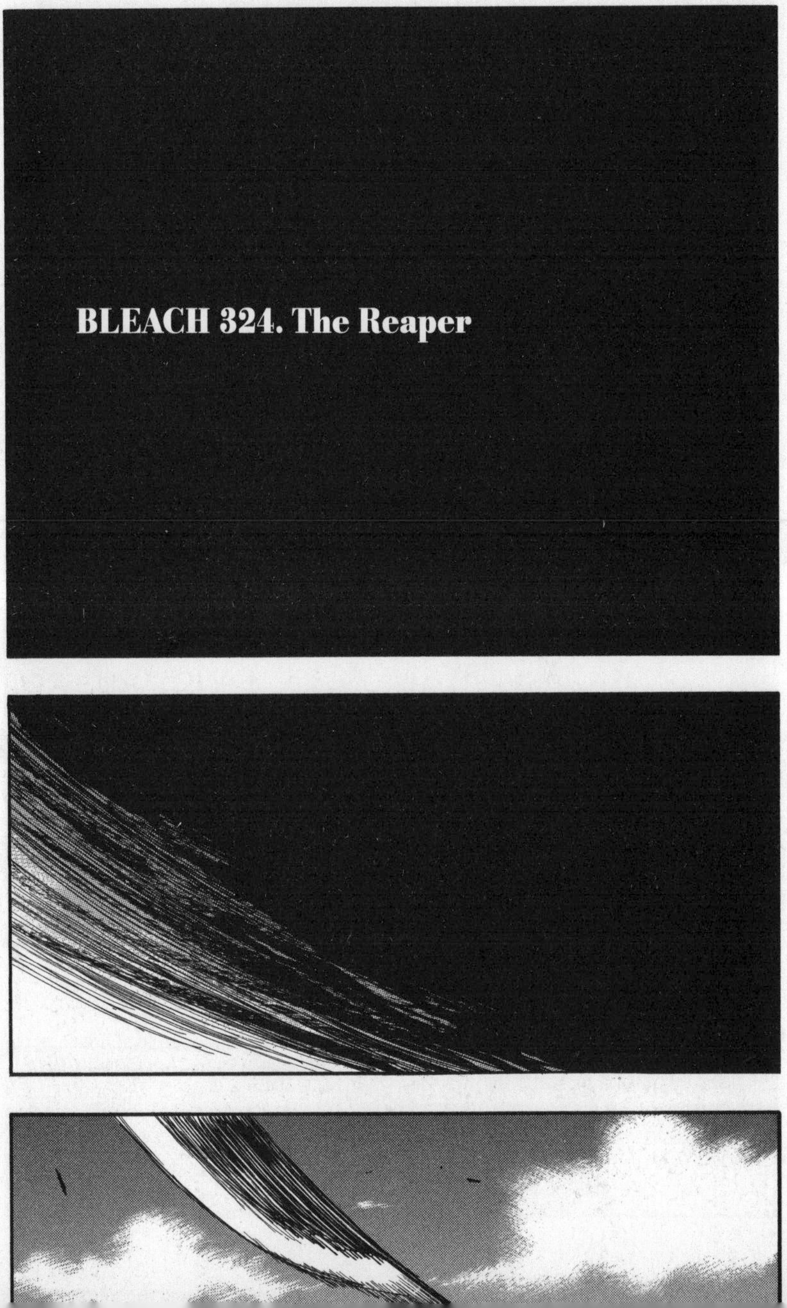
BLEACH 324. The Reaper

FWIP
WHAT'S WRONG, ASSISTANT CAPTAIN?!
YOU LOOK EXHAUSTED!
WHY WOULD FIGHTING ANOTHER ASSISTANT CAPTAIN WEAR YOU OUT SO?

DOOM
HOW CAN THIS BE?!
YOU'RE TIRED AND I'M NOT.
AFTER ALL, WE'RE BOTH AT THE SAME LEVEL.
WHY DO YOU THINK THAT IS?!

SHUT UP.
YOU THINK I'M NOT FIT TO BE AN ASSISTANT CAPTAIN?
EXACTA!
VERY GOOD...
...ASSISTANT CAPTAIN!
IF I'VE CALCULATED YOUR STRENGTH CORRECTLY...
...IT MEANS EXACTLY THAT!
DON'T CALL ME ASSISTANT CAPTAIN.
I TOLD YOU MY NAME IS...
...SHUHEI HISAGI.
FORGIVE ME.
HOW CARELESS OF ME.
IT WAS RUDE OF ME NOT TO INTRODUCE MYSELF.

I AM ...
... FINDORR CALIUS.
...ONE OF KING BARRAGAN'S FRACCIÓNES ...
WELL...
NOW THAT WE'VE EXCHANGED PLEASANTRIES...
...LET'S SETTLE OUR DUEL ...
...THE WAY YOUR PEOPLE DO.
IN OTHER WORDS ...
...I'M GOING TO KILL YOU...
...SHUHEI HISAGI !!
CARVE UPON THE WATER ...

PINZA AGUDA.
(SHARP PINCER)

READ THIS WAY

69

EXACTA!
YOU ELUDED THE SONÍDO WELL!
ENOUGH WITH THE EXACTA CRAP!
LIFE IS A SERIES OF DIFFICULT CHALLENGES!
ONLY THOSE WHO MAKE THE CORRECT CHOICES SURVIVE!
SO IT'S ONLY NATURAL FOR US TO WANT TO MAKE AS MANY CORRECT DECISIONS AS WE CAN!
AM I WRONG?!
SO YOU'RE SAYING YOU HAVE ALL THE RIGHT ANSWERS?

KLINK
YOU CERTAIN-LY TALK BIG.
VS
H
POP POP POP POP POP POP
AGH!

READ THIS WAY
WOOOOOOO
BINDING SPELL 62...
HYAPPO RANKAN. (HUNDRED-STEP BALUSTRADE)
BOOM

IT'S OVER, BIG MOUTH.
YOU THINK SO, SOUL REAPER ?!

SHOOM
!
SHAK

A HIGH-PRESSURED STREAM OF WATER?!
EXACTA!
BUT IT'S NOT WISE TO TAKE YOUR EYES OFF YOUR ENEMY!
WHUP
NO ES EXACTA.
I'M SORRY, SOUL REAPER!
WOOSH

WHUP
YOU THINK YOU DODGED IT?
SHWUD
SHWUD SHWUD
BOOM

REAP...
...KAZESHINI.
(DEATH WIND)
SHLAK

WIP
WIP
WIP
WHAP

I WONDER IF THAT THING ON HIS NECK IS A BOMB TOO.

325. Fear For Fight

SO THAT'S YOUR ZANPAKU-TÔ...
...SHUHEI HISAGI.

YES.
THIS IS KAZESHINI ...
...MY ZANPAKU-TÔ.
ALTHOUGH...
...I DON'T LIKE IT VERY MUCH.
...?
WHAT DO YOU MEAN?
JUST WHAT I SAID.
I DON'T LIKE THE SHAPE.
SHANK
LOOK AT IT.

IT'S SHAPED LIKE SOME-THING...
...DE-SIGNED TO TAKE LIVES.
SHUDDER
CHANK

BLEACH 325. Fear For Fight

READ THIS WAY

SHAK
AH...
WH

KLANG
WHOOM
CHAK

CHANK
COME BACK HERE!!
TUG

ZAN
SHLAK
TUMP
UN-PREDICT-ABLE, ISN'T IT?

WIP
HE WHIPS AROUND WILDLY.
WIP
WIP
WRR
WRR
WRR
AFRAID?
PLEASE !!

SWA
SH
NO ?
WELL, I AM.
TUG
W
AFRAID ?!
AFRAID YOUR POWER IS TOO GREAT?!
HOW VAIN!
YOU MUST HAVE A GUILTY CONSCIENCE, SOUL REAPER!
SNIK
DOSHH
BUT I'LL RELIEVE IT!
RIGHT NOW!
SHEK

KA
KEKK
IT'S OVER!
YOU HAVE NO CHANCE AGAINST ME NOW !!
WITH 90 PERCENT OF MY MASK REMOVED, MY POWERS...
...ARE EQUAL TO THOSE OF A CAPTAIN !!

SHUK
!!
SO...
YOU'RE NOT AFRAID OF YOUR OWN STRENGTH...
WIP
WIP
...OR YOUR ENEMY'S.
FIGURES.
THOSE WHO DON'T FEAR THE BLADES THEY WIELD...
...DON'T DESERVE TO WIELD THEM.

THAT'S WHAT...
...I WAS TAUGHT.
B— BLAST!
TMP
SO NOW YOU'RE AFRAID.
CHANK
YOU'RE FINALLY MY EQUAL.

WOOOH
AAAAAAAAAAAAAH!!
WOOOOSH
ALL THAT TALK ABOUT BEING THE EQUAL OF A CAPTAIN ...
GIMME A BREAK.
SHWAK

DO

XROOM
THE PILLAR ...
...COLLAPSED !!
ONE OF US LOST ?!
WHO?!
I—
IKKAKU!!

326. Knockdown Monster

BLEACH326.
Knockdown Monster

MADA-
RAME'S
BEEN...
...DE-
FEATED
?!

ONE...
...DOWN.
RRMMMMM
IKKAKU!!

WHAP
STOP!
WHAT CAN YOU DO AGAINST SOMEONE WHO DEFEATED MADARAME?
YOU THINK I CARE?!
LET GO OF ME!!
WHUP
DOP

TMP
THAT'S NOT THE WAY A FIFTH SEAT SPEAKS TO A SUPERIOR.
I KNOW YOU'RE UPSET, BUT CONTROL YOURSELF.
KIRA...
THUD
DON'T WORRY.
IT WAS A GATEN.
SWOO
SWOOOO-OOO

!!
TENSÔ KAIKI... (REGRESSION TRANSFER)
WITH ONE OF THE PILLARS DESTROYED, THE REAL KARAKURA WILL START TO COME BACK!
WOOOOOO
SO THE TOWN'S COMING BACK NOW...

I THOUGHT BALDY HERE WAS HOLDING SOMETHING BACK.
I GUESS I'LL NEVER KNOW, NOW THAT HE'S DEAD.
WHAP
WHO'S DEAD?
DON'T GET AHEAD OF YOURSELF.
SHAKE
TOMP

READ THIS WAY

WHAM
WHA...

WHA-
BAM
THOOM
KRASH
CAP-

THOOM
CAPTAIN KOMAMURA!!

TETSU-ZAEMON!
YES, SIR!
TUMP
KLANK
HA!
OM
CHUNK
SW
O-O-OOOOOOOO

I'VE STOPPED THE REGRES-SION.
THEY'RE ONLY A TEMPORARY FIX, BUT IF WE'RE CAREFUL NOT TO BREAK THEM WHEN WE FIGHT, THEY SHOULD HOLD.
WHAP
IBA...
POH HA HA HA HA HA HA HA!!
WHUP

THUD
BOOM
TMP
HE'S BIG-GER THAN ...
...CAP-TAIN KOMA-MURA.
THAT WAS PRETTY GOOD, SOUL REAPER.
WAIT, ARE YOU A DOG?
KRAK
ANYWAY, THAT PUNCH WAS PRETTY GOOD.
BUT...

IT WASN'T ...
WHUP
...A REAL PUNCH!

SHROOSH
NOW THAT'S...
...A REAL PUNCH.
C-
CAPTAIN KOMAMURA!!
AND...
SWUFF
...WHILE I'M AT IT...
...I'LL SHOW YOU...
SHH K
...THE ULTIMATE PUNCH.
BREATHE...
...CALDERÓN.
(GREAT WHALE)

PLUMP
?!
POP
PLUP
SKWEEK
BOING
POP
W—
WHAT THE...
THUMP
BLUMP

DOOOM
PHEW...
CRUSHING YOU IS A REAL PAIN.

WHAT KIND OF LAUGH IS "POH HA HA HA HA," ANYWAY?

WOOOOOOOO
327. Knockdown Monsters
SHA
SHH
W—
RRMMMMMMMM
WHAT THE...
...BLAZES?!
RRMMMMMMMMM

PHEW...
CRUSHING YOU IS A REAL PAIN.

WHOA ...
WHAT A FREAK!
H—
HEY! IBA?!
WHERE WE GOING ?!
SHUT UP!!
THAT GUY SENT THE CAPTAIN FLYING!! WE WOULDN'T STAND A CHANCE AGAINST HIM!!
HUH ?!
WHAT COWARDLY LOGIC IS THAT?!
UGH ...
I FEEL BLOAT-ED.
SWAY

BUT...
...WHAT CAN I DO?
IT'S KING BARRAGAN'S...
...ORDERS!!
WHOOSH

LET GO OF ME, IBA!!
I'M SLOWING YOU DOWN!!
I SAID, SHUT UP!!
WAAAAAH!!

WHAT?!

GRR...
KREEEK
KREEK
KREEK
URGHHHHHH...
KRK KRK KREEK
RIO
KRAAAAA!!

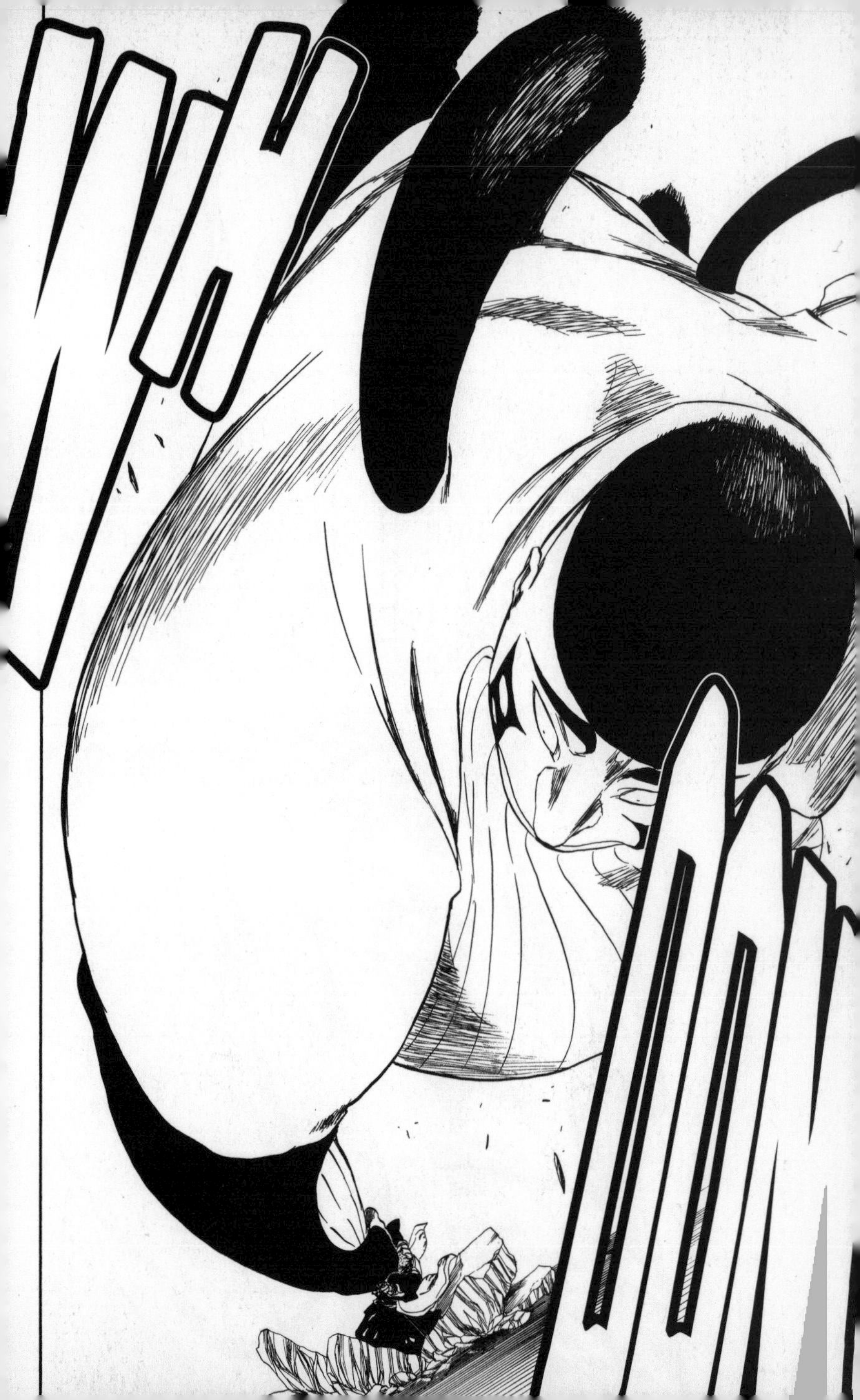

THOOM
HUFF
CA—
HUFF
CAP-TAIN!
NEVER RUN AWAY, TETSU-ZAEMON.
EVER.

STAND...
...BE-HIND ME.
YES, SIR!!

BLEACH 327. Knockdown Monsters

KRAESH
POH HA HA HA HA HA HA HA!!
THAT DIDN'T HURT A BIT!!
BUT IT DOES SURPRISE ME...
SWF
...THAT A BUG LIKE YOU...

...COULD THROW ME...
...ONE OF KING BARRAGAN'S FRACCIÓNES.
IT WAS SO SUR-PRISING ...
...IT'S MAKING ME YAWN.
KREEEEEEEEEEEEE
I SEE.
THEN ALLOW ME...
...TO STOP YOUR YAWN.
BANKAI.

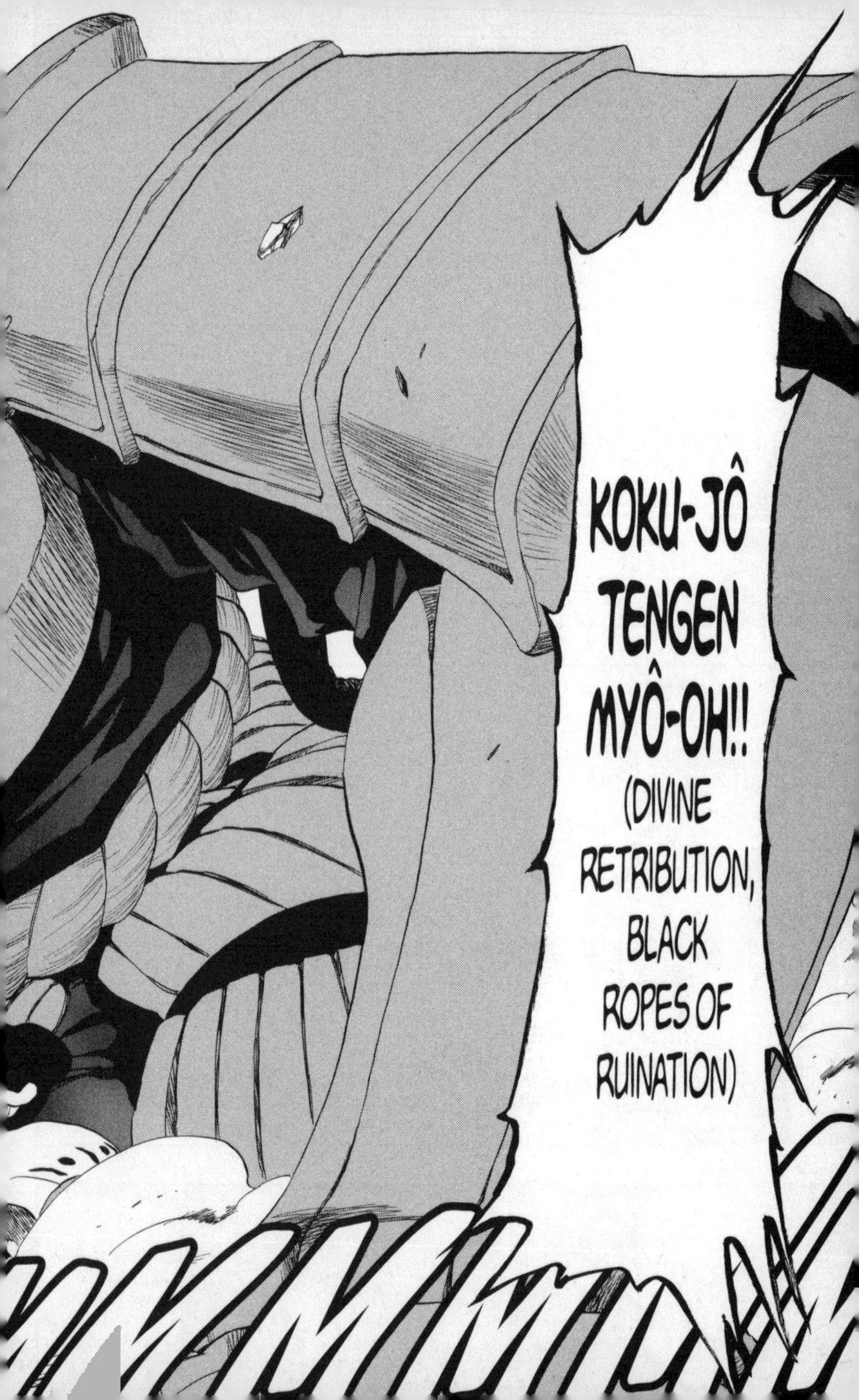
KOKU-JÔ TENGEN MYÔ-OH!!
(DIVINE RETRIBUTION, BLACK ROPES OF RUINATION)

RRMMMM

HUH?
WMMMMM MMM
THOOM
RRMMM MMM
WHAT ...
WHAT IS IT ?!
... ARE ...
... YOU ?!
RRMMMMMMMMMMM
WHAT...

THAT'S RIGHT.
I HAVEN'T INTRO-DUCED MYSELF YET.
I AM SAJIN KOMAMURA, CAPTAIN OF SEVENTH COMPANY.
AND, AS YOU SAY...

...I'M JUST A BUG OF A MAN.

No. 32
CHOE NENG POWW

328. The Knuckle Debate

328. The Knuckle Debate

BLEACH

BLEACH
ブリーチ

WHAM

KROO.....SH..
WHOA...
TALK ABOUT NO MERCY.
GOOD.

I GUESS IT DOESN'T MATTER WHETHER IT'S THE REAL KARAKURA OR THE REPLICA.
SEVENTH COMPANY'S GOING TO BE IN DEBT EITHER WAY.
A GOOD CAPTAIN PAYS FOR THE DAMAGES HIS SUBORDINATES CAUSE.
THAT'S WHAT KOMAMURA DOES.
SERI-OUSLY?! GREAT!
NOW I CAN FIGHT WITH TOTAL ABANDON?! ♪
NO YOU DON'T.
I'M TAKING EVERYTHING YOU BREAK OUT OF YOUR PAYCHECK.
I'M SORT OF GLAD... WE DIDN'T MAKE IT IN TIME.
YEAH.
WHOOSH

THU...D
SWIP

FWOOF
OF COURSE.
AMAZ-ING...
...

IT'S NOTHING LIKE YOUR BANKAI...
...EH, IKKAKU?
IBA...
DON'T YOU THINK I KNOW, FOOL?
...
RELAX.
I WON'T TELL THE CAPTAIN.
BUT...
...YOU SHOULD THINK HARD ABOUT THIS, IKKAKU.

IT WAS YOUR DUTY TO PROTECT THE PILLAR...
...BUT YOU ALLOWED IT TO BE DESTROY-ED.
DO YOU KNOW WHY?
IT'S BECAUSE YOU HELD BACK.
YOU'RE WELCOME TO GET YOURSELF KILLED ON YOUR OWN ACCOUNT.
HOW-EVER...
...DUTY MUST ALWAYS COME FIRST!
AND NEVER ALLOW PERSONAL STUBBORN-NESS...
...TO UNDERMINE THE COMPANY'S MISSION.
ORDERS IN THE THIRTEEN COURT GUARD COMPANIES ARE AB-SOLUTE.
THEY MUST BE CARRIED OUT...
...EVEN IF IT MEANS SWALLOW-ING YOUR PRIDE!
IBA...
I REALIZE THAT! I JUST...

UGH!
SHRUFF

YOU KNOW NOTHING, BOY.
DO YOU THINK THIS IS A GAME?
TMP
IF YOU GOT KILLED, SOME-BODY'D REPLACE YOU.
THAT'S WHAT YOU THOUGHT, ISN'T IT. THAT'S WHY YOU ALLOWED YOURSELF TO LOSE.
NOW, HOLD ON.
KLAK
IS THAT WHAT YOU THINK?
YOU THINK I LET MYSELF LOSE?
THAT'S RIGHT.
DIDN'T YOU?
YOU JERK!!

KREEK
A STRAIGHT-FORWARD ATTACK ...
WHA
...IN YOUR CONDITION?
THUD
IT'S OBVIOUS YOU'RE NOT REALLY FIGHTING TO WIN!
BUT YOU HAVE TO WIN, EVEN IF IT MEANS RETREATING OR SNEAKING UP FROM BEHIND!
NO! I WON'T FIGHT LIKE A COWARD !!

THEN GET STRONGER !!
IF YOU WANT TO FIGHT FAIR, THEN PAY THE PRICE.
I EXPECT YOU TO WIN NO MATTER WHAT THE COST.
!
IT'S CALLED...
...PUTTING DUTY FIRST.

CAP-TAIN...
TWITCH
EH?
DON'T WORRY.
TMP
UN-FORTUN-ATELY...
...MY HEARING'S NOT THAT GOOD TODAY.

RRMMMMMMMMM
THEY ALL... LOST...
IDIOTS!
KRASH
KREEK!

WHUP
WE'RE SORRY, KING BARRAGAN!
WE'LL FINISH IMMEDI-ATELY.
SIT DOWN, PLEASE!
TMP
FINISH WHAT?

READ THIS WAY

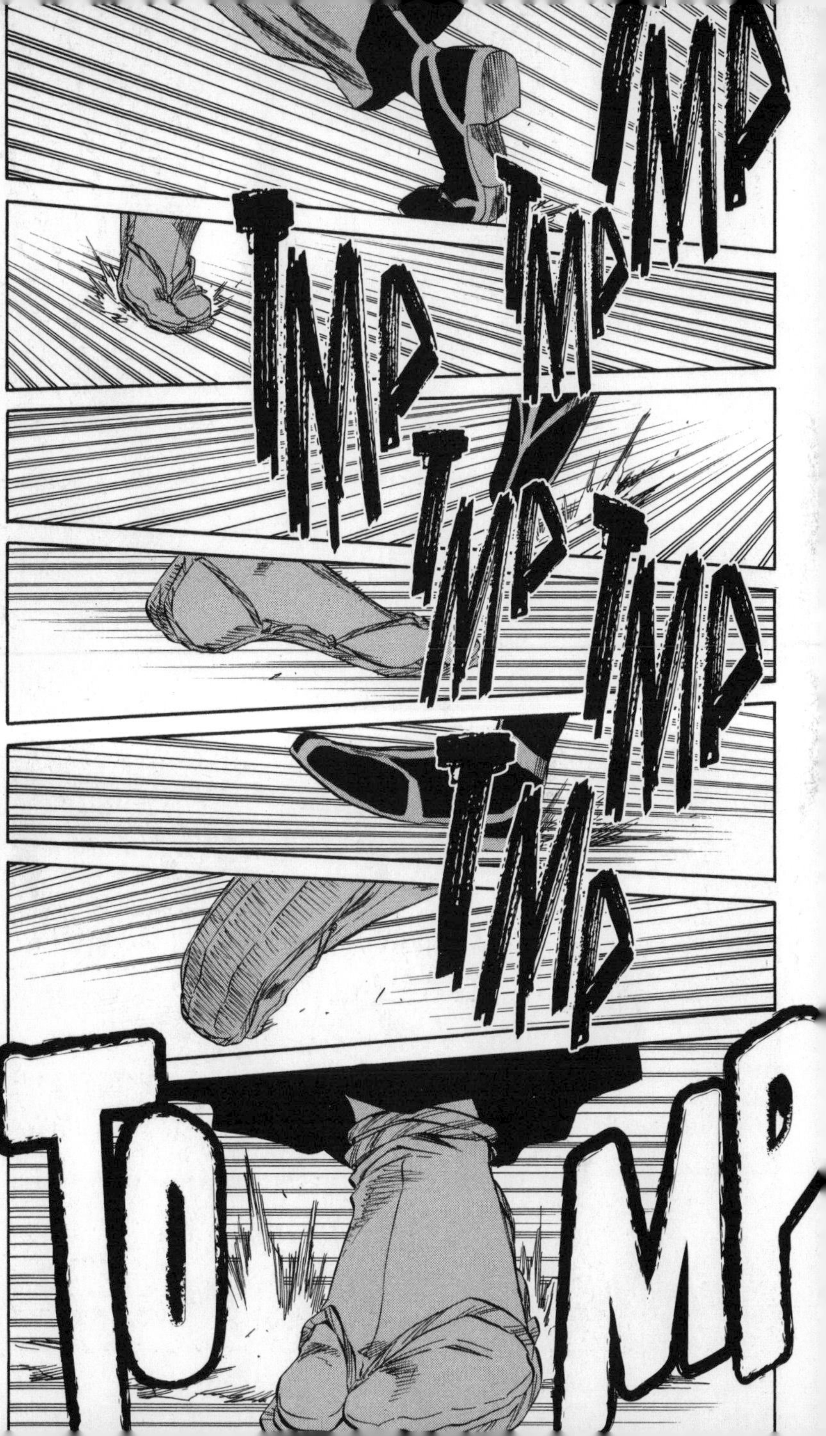
TMP
TMP
TMP
TMP
TMP
TMP
TOMP

THE CURTAIN...
TUNK
NOW THEN...
...HAS FINALLY BEEN RAISED.

SORRY, GORO.
I CAN ONLY
AFFORD TO
FEED YOU
OKARA
(SOY PULP)
THIS MONTH.

329. RAGING RAMPAGE

ATTACK

READ THIS WAY

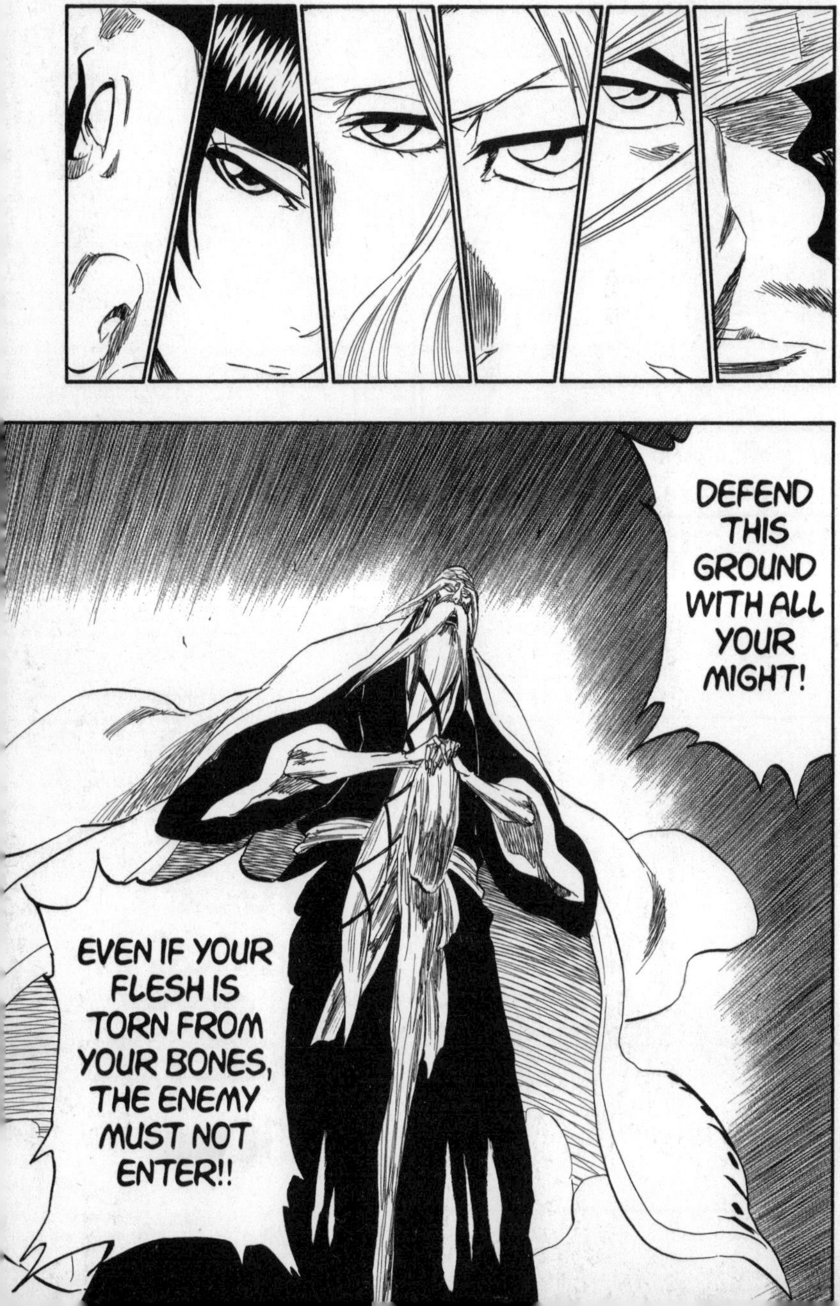

DO NOT ALLOW THEM...
...TO SET ONE FOOT ON SOUL SOCIETY SOIL!
OH, DEAR. IT MAKES ME TENSE...
...TO BE AROUND OLD MAN YAMA...
...WHEN HE'S LIKE THIS.
I KNOW.
WHEN THIS IS OVER, WE SHOULD RUB HIS SHOULDERS LIKE WE USED TO.

NO, NO.
MY SHOULDERS ARE THE ONES THAT NEED RUBBING.
WHAT ARE YOU TALKING ABOUT?
I'VE NEVER KNOWN YOU TO WORK ENOUGH TO GET TENSE SHOULDERS.
SHAKE
HUFF
OMA-EDA!
HUFF
YOU'RE TOO STIFF.
YOU'RE SCARED. YOU HAVEN'T BEEN IN COMBAT FOR A LONG TIME.
YOU'RE SO PATHETIC I CAN BARELY LOOK AT YOU.
THIS IS A GREAT OPPORTUNITY.
YOU SHOULD GET YOURSELF KILLED AS SOON AS POSSIBLE.
WHAT ?!
HA HA! WHAT ARE YOU TALKING ABOUT ?!
I'M NOT STIFF OR SCARED!
AND NOBODY'S GONNA KILL ME!!

IS THAT SO?
THEN DON'T GET KILLED.
YOU DON'T HAVE TO TELL ME THAT!
IT'S STARTING...
...MATSU-MOTO.
IS THERE ANY DOUBT IN YOUR HEART?
WHAT ARE YOU TALKING ABOUT?

NEVER MIND.
LET'S GO.
STAY SHARP, MATSUMOTO!
TMP
YES, SIR!

BLEACH
329.

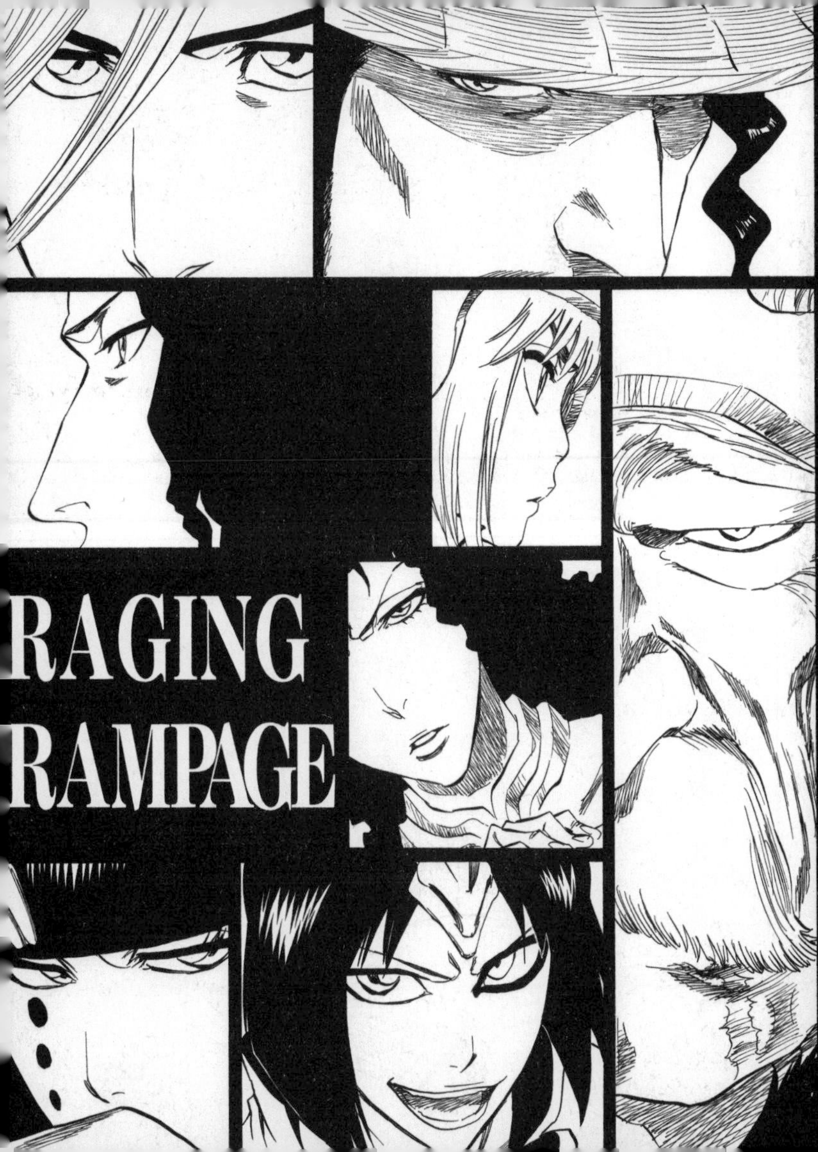
RAGING
RAMPAGE

KILL THEM.
DON'T LEAVE ANY OF THEM ALIVE.
IF YOU FAIL, YOU'LL HAVE NO HOME TO RETURN TO...
DO NOT DISAPPOINT ME.

DRENCH THE GROUND...
...WITH THE BLOOD OF OUR ENEMIES.
SAY IT!
WHO DO YOU SERVE ?!
SIR!
WE ARE KING BARRAGAN LUISENBARN THE GREAT'S FRACCIÓNES!
TMP

WE WILL ANNIHILATE OUR ENEMIES ...
...AND COVER THIS BATTLE-FIELD...
...WITH THEIR BLOODY CARCASS-ES.
WOOOOO
THE CHILD...

WOULD YOU MIND...
...SEND-ING HER AWAY FROM HERE?
...
WHY?
I CAN'T FIGHT MY BEST WITH HER AROUND.
ISN'T IT THE SAME FOR YOU?
WHAT?!
BE STILL, LILINETTE.
THAT'S FINE...
NO NEED TO FIGHT YOUR BEST.
WE CAN JUST PLAY AROUND.

WHAT DO YOU MEAN?
THIS GOES AGAINST ...
...MY NATURE.
IF I HAD MY WAY, WE'D JUST PRETEND TO FIGHT AND LET THE OTHERS DO THE REAL FIGHTING.
WHAT ARE YOU ...
I LIKE IT!!
NO, REALLY! I'D MUCH RATHER DO THAT TOO!
I DON'T LIKE PAIN!
BUT...
TMP
NOT THIS TIME.
I CAN'T.
I SEE.

SHHK
HOW REGRETTABLE.
WHUD
CAPTAIN...
I'LL TAKE CARE OF THESE THREE.
YOU TAKE THE ESPADA IN THE BACK.
CAN YOU HANDLE THIS?
I CAN.
WMM
ALL RIGHT.
I'M COUNTING ON YOU.

YOU'RE NOT GOING ANY-WHERE!
SWUP
ZANG
WAIT!
TMP

SHK

No. 27
NIRGGE PARDUOC

330. CROSSING SWORDS

WHAP
SWI

CHAK
CHAK
KREEK
TMP

BLEACH
330.
CROSSING SWORDS

THAT PIG!!
HE DREW HIS SWORD ON LADY HALIBEL!!
WAIT, APACHE!!
LATER!
ARE YOU INSANE, MILA ROSE?!
DO YOU WANT THAT RAT TO HARM LADY HALIBEL?!
FOOL.
LADY HALIBEL DREW HER SWORD.
THAT GRAY-HAIRED KID DOESN'T STAND A CHANCE.
IF YOU WANT TO HELP HER OUT...
...DO IT AFTER WE TAKE CARE OF THIS WITCH RIGHT HERE.
RIGHT.
SHE DID SAY...

WOOOOOOO
...SOMETHING ABOUT...
...TAKING CARE OF ALL THREE OF US.
HMPH.
YOU HAVE GOOD EARS.
I WAS AFRAID YOUR HEARING WAS AS BAD AS YOUR FACE AND SENSE OF STYLE.
WHAT DID YOU SAY ?!
TUG
SHE'S TRYING TO PRO-VOKE YOU.
DON'T FALL FOR IT.
THAT'S RIGHT.
LISTEN TO THE SHE-GORILLA.

WHAT DID YOU SAY?!
WHO'RE YOU CALLING A SHE-GORILLA, YOU MILK COW!!
STOP IT, YOU TWO. YOU'RE EMBARRASSING YOURSELVES.
SHE WANTS YOU TO LOSE YOUR TEMPER.
I REALIZE YOU'RE BOTH INCOMPETENT, BUT DON'T DRAG ME INTO THE MUD WITH YOU.
GRAH!
WHOSE SIDE ARE YOU ON, SUN-SUN?!
WHAT A COINCIDENCE.
I WAS JUST THINKING THAT YOU TWO WERE GETTING IN MY WAY.
WE CAN CLOBBER YOU FIRST IF YOU WANT!!
HUH?!
THEY'RE SO FUN TO TEASE.
CHAK
IT'S A LITTLE LATE TO LOOK TOUGH.
YOU SHOULD'VE SURROUNDED ME.
THE MOMENT YOU THREE CLUMPED TOGETHER, YOU LOST YOUR TACTICAL ADVANTAGE.

SHWO
...
GROWL ...
...HAINEKO.
(ASH CAT)

READ THIS WAY
FWOOSH
WHAT'S THIS?!
YOU WITCH!
YOU THINK YOU CAN BEAT US WITH SAND?!
TUMP
AGH!
WHAT WAS THAT FOR?!
DON'T TOUCH THINGS YOU KNOW NOTHING ABOUT!
YOUR STUPIDITY IS BREATH-TAKING.
CHAK
WHAT?!
WHAP
SWOP

AH!!
APACHE !!
CHAK
THAT'S HAINEKO'S POWER.
ITS BLADE TURNS TO ASH ...
...AND CUTS WHATEVER IT TOUCHES.
THINK OF THE ASH SURROUND-ING YOU...
...AS MY SWORD.

THERE'S NOWHERE TO RUN.
SKWIK
VWMM
!
WHUP
WHOOSH
BE CARE-FUL.
THE ASH IS SPINNING AT HIGH SPEED.
IT WILL SHRED ANYTHING IT TOUCHES.

NOT SO FAST.
YOU THINK THAT'S ENOUGH TO BEAT US?

KA-BUO
DID YOU REALLY THINK ...
...YOU COULD TAKE US OUT WITH THAT GIMMICK ?!
AH ...
SHOO
HAINEKO !!

WHAP
HUH ?!
HEH HEH HEH HEH !!
WHUP
HUH ?!
HA HA !!
UGH!

AREN'T YOU WOR-RIED?
YOUR COMRADE'S GETTING HIS BUTT KICKED BACK THERE.
I DON'T CARE.
ALL THAT JACKASS CARES ABOUT IS FOOD, MONEY AND HIS FAMILY BUSINESS.
IT'LL BE GOOD FOR HIM TO GET ROUGHED UP A LITTLE.
WHAK
WHAK
WHOA.
YOU'RE COLD.
CAMARADERIE IS OVERRATED.
A HEALTHY RIVALRY BETWEEN OFFICERS AND SUB-ORDINATES IS BETTER. IT KEEPS THE COMPANY SHARP.
WHAK
WHAK
HMPH.

WAP
SHWUP

R—
RATS!
SWUSH
BINDING SPELL 30...
SWIP
SHITOTSU SANSEN. (TRIPLE-FLASH BEAK SLASH)
SHUN
SHUN

READ THIS WAY

THE TECHNIQUE OF WRAPPING ONE'S ARMS OR LEGS AROUND AN ENEMY STRIKE AND USING IT AS A PIVOT OF ATTACK IS CALLED TSURI GAKI. (HANGING PERSIMMON)
IT WAS ORIGINALLY DEVELOPED BY LADY YORUICHI. WATCH CLOSELY!

331. Don't Believe the Hide

YOU'LL FIND OUT SOON ENOUGH.
KLIK
TUMP

WHAP
!
CERO!
ZH
EEN

AGH!

READ THIS WAY

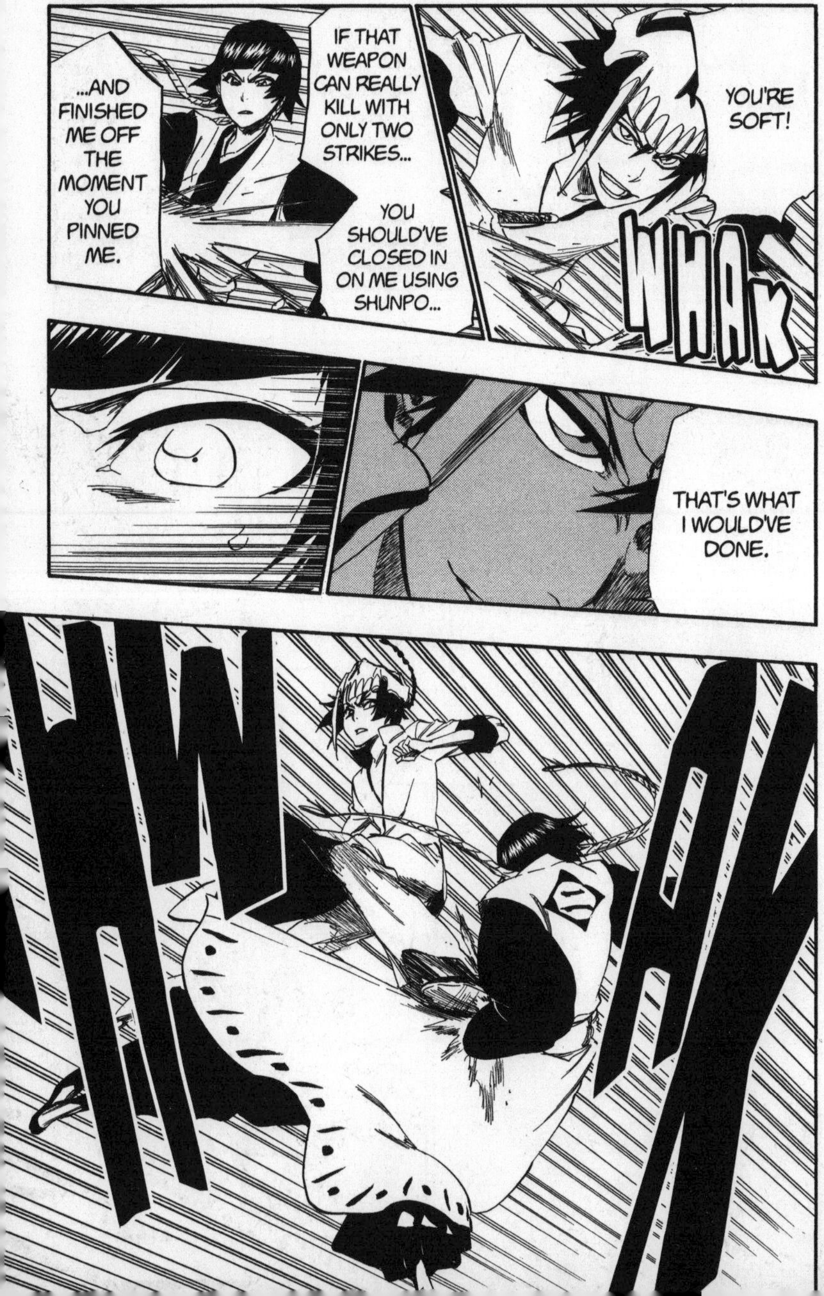

KROOOM
YOUR INSIGNIA SAYS YOU'RE THE CAPTAIN OF SECOND COMPANY.
YOU'RE THE SECRET REMOTE SQUAD, RIGHT?
KLAK
I HEARD THAT WAS AN ASSASSIN UNIT, BUT...
...YOU FIGHT LIKE AN AMA-TEUR.
KLAK
OR IS THIS LITTLE DANCE WHAT PASSES ...
...FOR AN ASSASSIN-ATION IN THE SOUL SOCIETY?

I'M HAPPY FOR YOU.
FWIP
YOU NOW HAVE TIME...
...TO LEARN MY NAME.
I'M GGIO VEGA...
...OF HIS MAJESTY KING BARRAGAN'S FRACCIÓNES.
AND WHILE I'M AT IT...
WIP
WIP
WIP
...I'LL TELL YOU...
...THE NAME OF THIS AS WELL.
WH AP
BITE OFF...
...TIGRE ESTOQUE.
(TIGER RAPIER)

BLEACH 331. Don't Believe the Hide

HAAAAAAAAH!!
AK
WH
HIYA!!
WHAK
HA!
WHAK
HIYA! HIYA! HIYA! HIYA!!
WHAK WHAK
HMF! HMF!
AK WHAK WHAK WHAK
HIYEEEE
YAAAAAA!!
WHAK WHAK WHAK
HUFF
HUFF
HUFF
HUFF

SWA
OOF !!
WHAM
THUMP
THUMP
THUMP THUMP THUMP
HMPH.
I REALLY...
...WANTED TO FIGHT THAT BLONDE LADY.
I'M NOT INTERESTED IN A SLOW FAT PIG LIKE YOU.
L—
LOOK WHO'S TALKING.
YOU'RE WAY FATTER THAN I AM!

READ THIS WAY

MAMUT.
(MAMMOTH)
BAAH!!
GEEZ! WHAT'S WITH THESE GUYS AND THEIR TRANSFORMATIONS?!
THEY'RE GETTING ALL HUGE...
...WHILE WE'RE JUST FIGHTING WITH SWORDS!

KRASH
WHAM
HO HO HO HO !!
MY RESURRECCIÓN FORM'S BULK MAKES ME A BIT SLOWER!
BUT IT'S JUST RIGHT FOR A FAT SLOB ...
THOOM
THOOM
...LIKE YOU!
THUD THUD THUD
THOOM
THOOM
HA HA HA !!
RUN, FATTY, RUN!!
TMP TMP TMP TMP TMP TMP TMP TMP
THOOM

WHOOM
TMP TMP TMP TMP
IDIOT!!
LEGS AREN'T IMPORTANT IN INNER-CITY COMBAT. QUICK THINKING IS!!
YOUR SIZE MIGHT BE AN ADVANTAGE GOING DOWNHILL, BUT IT'LL BE ROUGH GOING UP! COME AND GET ME!
THUD
WAAAAAH!!
THAT'S NOT FAIR!!
YOU SHOULDN'T BE ABLE TO JUMP THAT HIGH!!
HAVEN'T YOU HEARD?
YOU SHOULDN'T JUDGE PEOPLE BY APPEARANCES.
WHAM

HOW...
...DID YOU...
WHO DO YOU THINK I AM?
I'M THE ASSISTANT CAPTAIN OF SECOND COMPANY AND CAPTAIN OF THE SECRET REMOTE SQUAD'S SECOND DIVISION, THE SECURITY FORCE UNIT...
...MARECHIYO OMAEDA !!
I'M WITH THE SECRET REMOTE SQUAD.
HOW COULD I BE SLOW?
SO YOU WERE ACTING!
BASTARD!!
WHUP

CRUSH
...
...GEGE-
TSUBURI!!
(FIVE HEADS)

LET THAT BE A LESSON TO YOU.
YOU SHOULDN'T JUDGE PEOPLE BASED ON...
...APPEARANCES.

CONTI
NUED
IN
BLEACH
39

Datos de Arrancar 1

QUATRO	RANK
Ulquiorra Schiffer	#4 クアトロ
	169cm 55kg
	Fracciónes:
	nada
	Resurrección:
	————
	Theme Music
	In Flames "Moonshield" from [The Jester Race]

SEXTA	RANK
Grimmjow Jeagerjaques	#6 セスタ

186cm
80kg

Fracciónes:

11: Shawlong Qufang
12: Edorad Leones
13: Nakim Grindeena
14: Ilfort Grantz
15: D-Roy Linker

Resurrección:

PANTERA

Theme Music

**Bomb LA
(A Bombs)
"Step Inside"
from
[And Just
Constantly
Rotating]**

eview

The battle now shifts to the captains as Soi Fon, Shunsui and even Captain General Yamamoto get in on the action! Meanwhile, Ichigo faces his own troubles back in Hueco Mundo!

Read it first in SHONEN JUMP magazine!

PHONE IN AND THEN...
...FIGHT TO GET OUT!
From the pages of SHONEN JUMP Magazine!
PSYREN
Story and Art by Toshiaki Iwashiro
PSYREN
1
Story and Art by Toshiaki Iwashiro
ISBN-13- 978-1-4215-3676-7
$9.99 US | $12.99 CAN
Ageha Yoshina just got transported to a warped alternate dimension where you've got to fight your way back to our world—or die trying.
SHONEN JUMP
MANGA
www.shonenjump.com
On sale now at
www.viz.com
Also available at your local bookstore or comic store.
PSYREN © 2007 by Toshiaki Iwashiro/SHUEISHA Inc.
RATED
T
FOR
TEEN
ratings.viz.com
viz media
www.viz.com